Ghosts Only I Can See

by
Julie Alden Cullinane

YELLOW ARROW
PUBLISHING
Baltimore, Maryland, USA

Library of Congress Control Number: 2024946023
ISBN (paperback): 979-8-9883176-4-7

Cover design and interior images by Alexa Laharty (Instagram
@alexaelisabeth). Cover photography by Julie Alden Cullinane
(Instagram @HerLoudMind). Overall design by Yellow Arrow
Publishing. For more information, see yellowarrowpublishing.com.

"Let me fall, if I must fall. The one I will become will catch me."
~Baal Shem Tov~

Table of Contents

Acknowledgments

Chapter House Literary Journal (online), February 2023
"Big Need"

Salmon Creek Journal, Spring 2023
"Gasoline Shampoo"

OPEN: Journal of Arts & Letters, April 2023
"The Porcelain God is Female"

Underscore_Magazine (online), May 2023
"The Red Line"

A Playlist Inspired by *Ghosts Only I Can See*

All songs mentioned here can be found on Spotify. Enjoy!

1. A-ha. "Take On Me."

2. Better than Ezra. "In the Blood."

3. Bleachers. "I Wanna Get Better."

4. Buckley, Jeff. "Hallelujah."

5. Christine and the Queens. "Tilted."

6. Cooke, Sam. "Bring It On Home To Me."

7. Counting Crows. "Omaha."

8. Fall Out Boy. "Sugar, We're Goin Down."

9. Florence + the Machine. "Morning Elvis."

10. Krauss, Alison. "Ghost In This House."

11. Lambert, Miranda. "Settling Down."

12. Maal, Baaba and Mumford & Sons. "There Will Be Time."

13. Minaj, Nicki. "Super Bass."

14. Nicks, Stevie. "Stand Back."

15. Queen and Bowie, David. "Under Pressure."

16. Rateliff, Nathaniel & The Night Sweats. "Hey Mama."

17. Simon, Paul. "The Obvious Child."

18. Springsteen, Bruce. "I'm on Fire."

19. Talking Heads. "This Must Be the Place (Naïve Melody)," (2005 Remaster).

20. The Lumineers. "Cleopatra."

21. The Replacements. "Can't Hardly Wait."

22. The Rolling Stones. "Beast of Burden."

23. The Roots. "The Seed (2.0)."

24. Van Etten, Sharon. "Mistakes."

Thank you to my sisters, who will always be a part of my stories.

Ghosts Only I Can See is dedicated to Mike, Michael, Aidan, and Mac—my cup runneth over.

And to JMA: I see you still. You come when I need you most, peeking around corners, laughing into the wind, writing your name anywhere that it will fit. Beautiful, wild, brave little thing.

GHOSTS ONLY I CAN SEE

Big Need

I see the sound of big need on my face
Mirrored in the sleek black glass window.

Its sicklewings spreading
Belt-buckle divot pressed into my forehead.

Like the pink half-moons of my thumb flesh
Sis is a furnace.

I'm sluicing anguish.
Greased up guts

Taste acid and horrible sour.
The slightest slight shatters me.

Two-hundred and fifty dollars an hour,
Three-degree therapist

My words a soupy, half-formed yolk
Ashamed of how wet they sound when I speak them.

She chews—neutralizes them and spits them back to me
In slime-soaked beige.

Now a signature, not a thumbprint.
When bad things happen,

Before bones and organs are finished
It's too late, they fossilize.

Then pay pay pay for careful extraction
Without nicking an artery.

She's a pixelated glitch in an armchair
A color with no smell.

The radiator is a kettle that can't come.
It stirs my blood.

You are terrifying in your happiness
Beautiful and awful.

Amongst all these unbearable bodies
A chemical hurt bubbles up at once, chokes me.

A sneak of a flame.
I swallow it, scribble yellow pad.

I want to vomit out the window and
Have it boomerang back into my throat
Clean.

Your promise was a lid
I gladly lived under.
Breathed through holes in the cardboard
Big eyes examining me.
A shrinking violet
A pharaoh once.

I Only Let Women's Hands in My Body

The day before I graduate from a large Catholic University, I'm lying on a cold metal table in a blue flowered hospital gown and pink socks. It's like an alien autopsy. I can see myself outside of my body as if my brain is flying above me like a drone filming memory. (I don't want to remember, though, and my recollections of this day are just flashes and quick scenes.) I had felt the need to fib on my way in as my six-foot-tall best friend cleared the way through the protestors on the sidewalk. "I just need birth control!!!" I screamed as I pulled my hood up over my head and ran into the waiting room of the Planned Parenthood clinic.

After the kind young doctor removes her warm gloved hands and her steel instruments from my uterus, she rolls the little OB-GYN stool next to my side. The last thing she does is hold my hand, and before I can even ask, she very calmly says, "You will be fine, you will be OK, someday you will have beautiful children when you want them." When you want them. She knew the burning question on my mind. I did not want kids that day on the table, but I did want them someday. I had barely survived getting out of my father's house with my life. I put myself into massive debt and worked three jobs while a full-time student at one of the best colleges in the country to get to this point. I was fighting to keep everything I went through hell to build, and for a future where my children and I would have good quality of life. I was not here on this table out of love. Love had not landed me here. There was no boyfriend in the waiting room hoping I was OK. I felt zero guilt. Even now, 30 years later, I do not look back with any guilt, despite the world doing its best to try and make it stick.

Today, we are losing the constant fight for women's rights to their own bodies. Roe vs. Wade was alive and well when I was a young woman in that clinic. Now the unthinkable overturn has made women criminals for choosing their own lives over going through a birth that could potentially kill them. Supportive doctors and nurses are powerless in some states to help them. Laws are ever-changing and decided by men with political power. Pro-life protests are a constant visual with billboards, TV commercials, and political speeches, all to shame us American women for making our own choices. I chose me then. I choose me now. My life. Young women today are not as lucky and that destroys me. I will never forget that kind young doctor and the feel of her smooth warm hands on mine.

~

Ten years later on another metal table, I am strapped down like Jesus in the shape of a cross. An older male doctor, who is not *my* doctor, has his hands in my uterus. He yells to anyone in the delivery room with ears, "She's bleeding out!" and I hear everyone calling for more blood. My husband is nowhere to be found. (He tells me after the fact that an RN had pulled him into a closet, thrown a pair of baby blue scrubs at him, and then asked him to sign some papers with checkboxes about whether he lets me or the baby die, or both.) Everything is blurry, and I can feel the life flowing out of me. "The baby, the baby, save my baby," I try to say, but no words move from my brain to my lips.

Suddenly and very cinematically, *my* OB-GYN bursts through the surgery doors, her blue surgery apron moving along with her in a flourish. Her hair is completely invisible under her surgeon's cap, but I see her beautiful eyes, and a part of me knows I am going to be OK. She struts in and tells the other doctor to step aside like a fucking X-Man. As I lose consciousness, I know I will be OK because she will put her hands into my nicked uterus, take out my son, sew me up, and save my life. She will firmly massage and coax my purple silent child back to me from across the veil and convince him to live while my intestines are neatly piled on my rib cage.

I wake up alone hours later in a very sunny and large hospital room. As my eyes start to focus, I immediately look at my stomach and see there is no longer a baby in there. I notice someone sitting at the foot of the bed, not next to it, but on it by my feet. Her hair is down and glistening like dark silk. She is in clean blue scrubs and sitting casually with one knee across her leg like a teenager. "Did you see my baby?" I ask her, proud but delirious with drugs. "Yes, he's beautiful," she says very seriously. "But I am most happy to see YOU here." I never felt more loved even though I know she means I am her patient, and she is glad that I am alive.

~

After two children, I am left with horrible teeth, and I never smile. I used to have perfect-perfect teeth, but my severe ADHD and previous dental trauma prevent me from getting treatment, let alone allow people to put their hands in my mouth. When I get my final cavity fixed, I will have a mouth without pain. After years of looking, I finally find a beautiful young red-headed genius at a dental school for people with mental and physical disabilities. She teaches me to wiggle my toes and shake out anxiety so that I don't notice her sticking six-inch needles into my jaw. She lets me hold a teddy bear and my childhood blanket as she cuts me open for implants. She laughs and tells stories about how she learned to use a microwave at 33 as she inserts four shiny screws perfectly into my jaw with her long gentle fingers. I welcome her hands in my mouth. She writes down a treatment plan with dates and says, "We will have you smiling again by Christmas." She convinces my insurance company that this is a serious medical procedure, and they pay for it. She gives me her personal cell phone number to call at any time in the next 48 hours to make sure I am OK and that there is no infection. She is out sick for the placement of my last implant. All the cutting has been done, the crown just needs to be measured and put in place.

I am assigned to a 65-year-old male dentist who, within five minutes of meeting me, has his hand on my right breast for most of the time he has a drill in his other hand. I dare not move or speak up because I don't want to ruin the beautiful teeth she has made me. He cuts my lip severely and gets the porcelain implant stuck in my jaw by muscling it into place. I sit up and stop him, and he gets mad. I say, "Let's stop here, and I will wait for Dr. X to come back from vacation." He is not thrilled. When he leaves, I ask the young student doctor to put in my chart that he is never to lay another finger on me as long as I am a patient here.

~

My perfect five-year-old son might lose his hearing after two years of continuous eardrum ruptures, failed tubes, and infections. We sit in the audio booth of the best Ear-Nose-Throat children's hospital in the world reading Elmo and waiting. When a middle-aged white-coat male walks in, he is cheery and kind, but my son scowls at him suspiciously. He crawls his little body up my side in defiance. "You are not a doctor!" he insists. The nice man bends down and says, "I am, see my stethoscope right here? I'm here to check your hearing." My son says politely but firmly, "No, you cannot be a doctor because you are not a lady." I turn red, but I smile with pride. "I'm sorry," I say, "it's just that in his short little life, every doctor he has ever met has been a woman." The doctor says to my son, "Well, aren't you a lucky guy?" He winks as he puts the sticker-covered headphones over my son's ears.

A Town for Worms

I fold my death neatly
And slip the small smooth white paper
Into my front jeans pocket.
I like all my options to be close
Near my warm skin and underclothes
So only I know it's there.
So no man can steal my secret.

I love the fall
The season of my life
But it's like bad fruit.
Summer's sloppy seconds
Sees everything rot.
Blood blossoms bleeding
Into a starved earth
Sucking in sustenance
For winter's starvation.

I imagine my dead body
As a town for worms
Brightly lit and crawling alive
Under my best black suit
As the green grass glees above.

Shades of Blue

She is never now or before
Not a memory or a hope
Even her smell is
The perfume of her future – a future
Love that is quick and sharp-clawed
Filled with people who can afford bad luck
Summer leaned on fall
Fall leaned on
Skin turned to tissue paper vague with fatigue
I rip at the slightest scrape

My waters were down
A shade of quiet ichor
The type of quiet you run from
A spoil of blue thread
A sewed-up bag of offal
Trying to be cool – aloof
Instead of feasting and fattening on laziness
I leaned over my hunger
Waited for it to pass
Buzzed with dizzy emptiness

She was the winter that lasted forever

When Ryan Gosling Lived in My Backseat

I don't remember when exactly Ryan Gosling started showing up in the backseat of my Ford Explorer. It was spotty at first, a day here, a day there, but then it was every day of my commute to Boston. As I look back now after a decade of expensive therapy, I can see how the events in my life at that time were simmering to a boil, and Ryan was just a hungry, empty ghost trying to help me escape. I had a high-demand life. There was too much of everything all at once and not enough peace.

The movie *Drive* had just come out when Ryan first showed up. It was strange because I didn't have a crush on or obsession with Ryan Gosling; he was just an actor to me. I had no emotional attachment to him, besides maybe that we were the same age and that I loved to drive. In *Drive*, he is the anti-hero, a mass murderer who we want to love and take under our wing because he sacrifices his life and sanity for the woman and child he loves.

Ryan always waited to appear until I dropped my two babies off at my mother-in-law's house to be watched during the day while I worked. He usually appeared right at the city limit, the point where I had mentally marked for years that I was leaving the suburbs and entering Boston. A long empowered parkway straight into the heart of the city. Back then, life was very stressful. I had two beautiful boys under three years old. I also had an undiagnosed miscarriage that I just plowed through and didn't want to think about. I had a taxing job in the city that took up most of my time. I did not want to work, but my husband and I were barely making ends meet, barely keeping the lights on, and my job had good health insurance for the boys. As lucky as I was to not have to pay for daycare, I almost never saw my children, and they were beginning to prefer my mother-in-law to me. It's funny because when I look back, I have no memory of where my husband, my sisters, or any of my family were in their lives back then. I know I was married and that my husband worked as well, but somehow, I have no recollection of him during that time. It was as if he was a ghost. I see it now, the isolation and lack of support, and how it led to these events.

I see myself with my hair pulled back in a bun, slicked at the sides and stretching my eyes up because it is so tight. I'm wearing my favorite maroon V-neck sweater because it made me feel more professional, like all the other women who spent millions on clothes at work. In my black Ford Explorer, Ryan would appear in his shiny *Drive* jacket, popped collar with a blue denim shirt underneath, bloodstains and all, black jeans, and sneakers. He would smirk and sit behind me with one ankle pulled up on his other knee, holding his shin to brace himself as he bounced along with the motion of the car. His eyes were constantly fixed on me. He also wore his maroon leather driving gloves.

For a while, an undocumented amount of time that could have been days, weeks, or months, Ryan and I never spoke. He just joined me on my daily commutes into the city, always sitting in the passenger side backseat. It was as if we communicated telepathically. I heard his thoughts in my head, and I spoke back to him this way. I felt evil when he was there. I have never felt as unsafe in my entire life, even now, as I did during those car rides with Ryan. It pains me to recollect those days even briefly because just the memory of how fraught my nerves were, how I was dripping with anxiety and fear, is enough to send me into a PTSD tailspin.

I decided I would ignore Ryan and that he would eventually go away. I knew if I told anyone, my husband, my parents, they either would do nothing or they might possibly take my children and leave me out on the streets. Looking back, they never would have, but I was not in the right frame of mind back then. I was in survival mode. Eventually, the cracks started to show.

Instead of being properly treated for my friend Ryan by a doctor, I took matters into my own hands. I thought back then that taking even one sick day would make me a bad employee, let alone taking a sick day to get help for my brain. I barely got six weeks maternity leave and couldn't afford to take any more vacation days. I didn't have time for that as I had a house, a husband, and children to take care of, as well as a job and bills. My right eye had begun to twitch, which I knew historically was a sign that I wasn't getting enough sleep and that things were about to pop off. The eye twitch was always a bad omen. I decided to borrow some Xanax from a friend to help me sleep, thinking that would solve everything. I was praying rest would make Ryan go away.

One very cold February morning, it took everything I had in me to go to work. I was a shell. My back and shoulders were on fire from anxiety and muscle tension. On the way to work, I snorted a Xanax, trying to be preemptive against the day's impending stress. There was so much snow already on the ground, and in Boston two flakes of snow was enough to cause a traffic jam for miles. I should never have left the house, but back then working from home was not an option. I looked in the rearview to see what Ryan advised, but I already knew the answer—drive!

Big mistake. I nodded off mid-commute and somehow got hit from behind, and it snapped me awake instantly. I remember looking into the rearview and there was Ryan, smirking. The guy that hit me did not speak English and as it turned out, he did not have car insurance, and neither did I. Mine had expired a week before without my knowledge. The Boston police came to haul us both off to jail. My car got towed with Ryan still inside.

They put me in a cell for about three hours. I knew they were probably running a background check that would find nothing. They gave me a big blue scratchy blanket. I could see my purse and cell phone just sitting on the officer's desk and hoped that was a good sign they were going to let me go. They said I wasn't charged with anything but asked if I wanted to make a phone call.

I declined. I didn't call work, I didn't call my husband, I didn't call my mother-in-law. I slept in the jail cell until they told me I was free to go. I never even checked if the cell door was locked. I was fully aware they were letting me go because of the color of my skin and the fact that I looked like a suburban housewife. I loathed myself at this point. I remember seeing the guy who rear-ended me being walked by my cell in handcuffs by two officers. I knew he was being charged and sent elsewhere. I wondered if the accident was my fault. Did I just screw this guy's life up forever? Did he have kids at home depending on him and his paycheck like me? I was fully saturated in shame and self-hatred. I lied to my husband. I told him I forgot to renew the car insurance, which was not a lie, but I left out most of the details. He was not mad; it was just another occurrence in our shitty life. He picked me up and drove me home in silence; he was beaten down as well. Ryan was nowhere to be found.

I got put on probation for three weeks the next day at work because no one could find me. I barely cared. I told them I got in a car accident, but my boss wasn't having it. I remember her saying, "There are such things as phones." I wished she would have fired me. I was begging to be put down. But no one would do it. A young white woman in her prime. A young mother. So much potential. They were giving me every chance to succeed, and they should have just let me fall.

The final straw came about two weeks later. I had been on my best behavior, but Ryan slowly crept back into my head. One night while heading home, it was so dark. Dark like Boston early in the winter when everyone who hasn't seen the sun in months turn into zombies. I have never done well when I wake up and go to sleep in darkness. It was snowing, and I couldn't see the road in front of me. It had been a long day, and I was eager to get back home to my children who I loved so much. I remember envisioning their beautiful, chubby little faces; they were such good babies, and thank God for that. Ryan was there, and the blood on his jacket was dripping extra red. He was smiling slightly, tapping the fingers of one hand on his knee and playing with a switchblade with the other. It was as if the world stopped. I remember the holiness and quiet of the winter-dark snow. The headlights were the only light I could see. My car was surrounded by its own little glorious blizzard of light and snow. I knew where I was by the street signs, and I remember Ryan's voice in my head. *It can all be over in a second. They are better off without you. The ravine is just one turn of the wheel. You will not feel a thing, I promise you.* His voice was so comforting and for once he wasn't mean or terrifying. I felt safe and loved, almost like he was trying to protect me.

I remember not being able to see through the blur of hot tears. I conjured up the feeling of the week before when I went to pick up my oldest son from my mother-in-law's, and he tried with his whole body to not go home with me. He wanted to stay with her because that's where he lived for almost 14 hours a day. I had to peel him off her and wrestle him into his car seat. I felt so ashamed and like such a failure. I loved him so much, maybe it would be better, better for everyone if I just disappeared. I clenched my hands so tight around that steering wheel that they hurt for days after. I didn't necessarily want to die, I just wanted it to stop. I wanted the hurt to stop, to just give me one minute of peace. I did not want to live in hurt any longer. I could feel my soul dying piece by piece every day. It was like slow organ failure. I knew I was dying.

I did not drive myself off a cliff and into a ravine. I pulled over instead and sobbed my guts out for about 20 minutes. The one thing I could not get past was that I would never hold my babies' warm fragile birdlike bodies close to me ever again and feel their fluttery little hearts against my chest. I would miss the warm brown sugar vanilla smell that little boys have, and three-teeth smiles and blond curls, and "mama" with wide open chubby arms. I spoke my first word to Ryan through mumbled sobs and sniffles. "No," I said. And that was the last time I ever saw him.

I quit my job a week later. I sat down with my husband and told him I would go back to waitressing nights because being away from the boys was slowly killing me inside. We would find a way to get health insurance. He agreed and started looking for a better job. I started seeing a therapist and getting medication.

I get angry now when I look back at that time. Angry at myself for not putting my health and well-being first, and angry that no one helped me or hauled me off to a mental facility. I wished and wished back then that someone would just pick me up and force me into one, but nobody did. I kept going like a bull through life, and I don't know how I did it. This is not a success story of survival. This should never have happened.

I understand now that Ryan wasn't *Drive*, and I wasn't me. We were both dangerous and chemical versions of ourselves, ticking and waiting to explode from neglect. Now that I look back that's probably why I manifested him; he was safe masculinity and then he wasn't, just as before I was safe femininity and then I wasn't.

I occasionally see Ryan Gosling movies now, although I change the channel immediately every time I see that *Drive* is on. Life is slower and because of the decisions I made there is far less pressure. I went back to graduate school and got a great job as a director at a hospital, where I mentor other women. I also teach creative writing to adults in the evening. I work from home four days a week in my 4000 ft² house. I can pay all my bills and write at my leisure; my boys are happy and healthy teenagers. Ryan is older now and more chiseled. He takes roles that walk the line between good and bad, kind of like me. He is married and has three beautiful girls of his own. We have a truce. We both stay alive.

How To Give Up Writing

Devolution, I've decided, another wolf that's gone dog
a mansion strewn with stains and empties

a body that feels filled with jagged-edged stones
instead of bread and a great, cheap burgundy

pages empty now, having chosen to lose
without ever experiencing a public, bare-breasted sword fight
I was once a good cold blade

it's like waiting to be pretty, to bloom into a demimondaine
starving a thin groin stretched in black fabric, a gaping space
between thigh meat

means when I was young and still had a graceful predator's body
I believed I could hear the whale song
the silk and bone of it

I'm like a mother who married out of exhaustion
folded herself away from scholarly risk like her
last educated dollar spent on

the wonderful feeling of walking behind a mammoth man
resting and hiding in his tall, wide shadow
from the doom and pet dread

left with the time
to rest and coagulate one crystal-clear thought

wait and watch for clouds with
 fat   bellies then
   low-hanging   reach my needle to the sky and prick to release
rain explosions
like swollen

rotten fruit
releasing
shimmering
silver
moths

once I kept my words tight
saved them in secret neatly stacked piles
until I could wipe them clean
        and fan them out in front of me
like white porcelain bathtub tiles
make them gleam like shiny pearl teeth.

The Red Line

I'm bleeding. I'm actually gushing. Panic sets in. I feel the adrenaline shoot into my nervous system from my right and left side like double-fired sidearms. I realize how much farther I must go before I can change my underwear, or at least my pad. I switched purses this morning at the last minute, and now the extra pad I so desperately need is safely in the purse at the bottom of my bedroom closet.

My period usually starts out a lot slower than this. Never all at once, or so fast. I'm not prepared, which is very unlike me. It's July, and I'm on the Red Line. Some people understand what that means without any explanation. I'm heading to a job interview that could change my life, my husband's life, my children's lives. There are the usual train zombies but also an unusual, oppressive heat. It's been 90 degrees all week. I'm sick of the sunshine. Today is no exception. My expensive outfit and blowout have long since wilted, my makeup melted. I'm waving the white flag before the battle even begins. *No, I have to get to this interview.* I mentally urge the train on and watch the doors between cars, expecting something to happen, except it doesn't. I keep thinking of *The Walking Dead* and wonder what it is about trains that always makes me think of that show and catastrophe.

To get to Cambridge, I have to go through all stops, the whole way. I ponder if I can superwoman jump out at South Station, grab a pad from the station bathroom and jump back on the Alewife line and still arrive on time.

I do it. I get off at South Station and beeline it to the ladies' room, which smells of humid marijuana and human sweat. The tampon and pad machine is empty. *Fuck.* I sit and let myself breathe for a moment on the toilet in the tiny metal stall. I can feel the thick gelatinous clots just sliding out of me, there's no end to them. I look into the toilet bowl, and it's a crime scene. I desperately try to clean up with wads and wads of toilet paper.

I wonder to myself how I can still be alive and upright with this much blood just pouring out of me. I imagine one of those old-fashioned glass milk bottles that we used to get delivered to my house when I was little, but full of blood, and I'm not sure why. Through the lock hole I can see another woman who is braiding her thick dark hair in a hurry and speaking an African language into her precariously balanced phone on the sink, which is on speaker. Whatever she is saying back to the person on the other end, I can tell she is having none of it. *Better not ask her,* I tell myself, she seems like she has her own shit going on today. I do what I can with the soaked-through pad and run back to the Red Line to grab the next train.

I get to the interview with 15 minutes to spare. I run for public bathroom number two of the day, hoping it is as stocked as I keep the women's bathroom at my current job. I do it as a courtesy for my students. A basket full of tampons and pads, breath mints, body spray, and dental floss, a small comfort in someone's day. Nope. Another empty machine. I feel the anger inject into my veins. I try AGAIN to clean myself up as much as I can. The blood has flooded into the thigh folds of my $147 new black pants, and I am so beyond thankful that I wore the black pants instead of the white this morning. It was a very close call. Both sides of my hands are covered in blood, and I'm delicately dancing with a roll of toilet paper, so I don't show up in my elegant white shirt covered in blood smears, looking like I just knifed someone on the train.

A group of giggling college students enters the bathroom. I think to ask them, but for some reason, I just can't; it's exhausting to even think about. They are all wearing super short denim shorts and tank tops as if it was a uniform. There is no way any of them are carrying a tampon. There is not enough fabric to hide a pad anywhere. I hold the door for an overheated young mom on her way into the ladies' room with two sleeping one year olds in a double stroller being carefully wedged through a too small doorway. Their bare little feet peek out from under a blanket. Only after the door closes do I visualize her open diaper bag. I seriously think about turning back and asking her for one. But I don't. *Am I the type of person to rob a young mom of her last diaper with twins?* Turns out I'm not.

I sit through coffee with a man who is, no joke, seven feet tall in an outdoor café with white metal furniture. I cross my legs and smile, trying to hide the discomfort. I can only see his outline against the glare of the sun. He asks if I am up for a short walk and a tour. "Sure" is all I can fake; I'm deep into my acting reserves. He is extremely nice, but the tour ends up being 11,000 steps by my watch's calculation. One of his strides equals three of mine.

Next, I'm sitting on a silky beige cushion on the rooftop deck restaurant of the Charles Hotel in Boston. We are having lunch outside in the heat for some reason instead of inside with gorgeous air conditioning. I'm facing an alpha female, my potential future boss. I've never had a lunch interview before. Eating in front of potential employers has got to be high up there on the intimidation tactics of interviews. I'm starving, but I sit like a stone, not moving or shifting. Holding myself together. I feel the blood spout every 10 minutes or so and pray that whatever is left of the absorption in my pad will prevent it from ruining the cushion I'm sitting on. A bee lands on my chicken club. She watches in horror and seems surprised by the fact that I don't jump and swat at it. *Fuck you bee*, is all I can think. I take two bites; I don't eat the side the bee landed on because there's silent judgment to see if I will eat the infected part. There are no pads in the hotel bathroom, even though my lemonade cost $12.

It's Friday afternoon, and the train home is flooded with too much human suffering. I know I am absorbing it. No one can bear to look at each other. Most just want to get home after a long week of work and take their armor off. I tip my head back against the window and let my sunglasses fall onto my face. I close my eyes and join the avoidance. It's ridiculously hot. My hair, skin, and clothes are drenched in sweat. I taste and smell my own salt and metal. I cradle my uterus with my right hand and guard my backpack with my left. I let the train rock me into a semi-conscious stifling trance.

Eight hours after leaving my house this morning and still wearing the same pad, I am finally safe in my own bathroom. I strip everything off, clothes, underwear, makeup, and jewelry. I cup the cold, crisp water from my faucet and suck it down. I flood my face with it and throw it over my shoulders, let it roll down my back and between my breasts. There's a loud knock on the door. I hear and see the doorknob turn from the other side, but I locked it. It's one of my teenage boys. "Mom, I need you in the garage. Can you come, please? Mom . . . you OK? You coming?"

I sigh and pat my face with a soft, clean towel. "Yup, give me one minute." I wait to hear the heavy footsteps retreat. I can tell he hesitates. I throw a navy-blue towel on the newly tiled floor and kneel to wipe the blood from the white grout where I was standing in front of the sink. It will stain permanently if I leave it. I sit back against the sharp coolness of the bathroom door. The cold steel makes my arm hair stand straight up. I close my eyes for one second and breathe in the cool air. Then I stretch to wipe the blood off my thighs and feet. I mentally remind myself to write thank-you emails later. I write the letters TY in blue pen on my thumb and head to the garage.

Coming of Age

You were best while still a sorrow
A ghost protesting
An auxiliary blanket
The twinge in my wings
You and the Major Arcana.

This age I've got has corners
No longer hidden by velvet ropes
Or doe-foot wands
Waving flesh-colored camouflage.

I need to satisfy the scream
Rivered in my ribs
Angled and spear-tipped
Let it draw clean lines
Around the silence.

Instead
A useless chipped roar
Is the lull before
My next devastation
Top heavy and heaving like
Donated disappointment
An intimate black
A hemmed shadow.

My spirit teeters on hinges
Squeaks without oiled joints
With one last silver-streak
Quick as a dog's bite
A bit
Bit bit itty bitty plot line left
Doesn't ease cleavage-deep burdens.

The Porcelain God is Female

Anything that takes bodily fluids into her swirling womb of cold water must be female, right? Shocking that it's called "the John" and not some female name like "the Lola" or "the Veronica" that you can buy in Home Depot. But hey, you know, men love to name things after themselves. Especially things as novel as a toilet. I mean, the porcelain goddess knows all, sees all. As a woman, a toilet is the goddess that watches over us from birth to death and all the ugly in between. Like how the woods and trees keep the forest's secrets, the toilet keeps ours. What is a more universal icon in a woman's life than a toilet? It's there for our violence, fear, happiness, and hatred, our mistakes and our illnesses. It sees all our fluids, tears, blood, urine, vomit, and waste. We seek its shelter and its judgment. It is there watching us from the beginning to the end of life. It's where we sit after sex to take a breath and wait for the semen to slide down from gravity so that we can wipe it away quickly before any infection can set in, or pull our knees up to hold it in in hopes of growing new life. We sit on the edge of her waiting for two pink lines or no lines, like a tarot card being turned over by a fortune teller; only what the toilet sees and tells will never lie. Where vigilance is constant for a rust brown or bright pink smear on the cottony whiteness signaling a UTI that will make us hazy and confused and in pain. Full of antibiotics that will fuck our gut for months on end, the toilet sees that, too. It sees us in the beginning, teetering our young over the cold ceramic edge so that we can teach them to be independent with their own bodily fluids, hoping that one day we will have one less chore to do. Except eventually we will have to teeter our old and elderly on that same cold rim. Bracing skinny arms and shoulders with our own, trying not to look the indignity right in their face.

We hug her in the best and worst of times while vomiting in penance for a night of drinking too much. We seek her solace in the throes of morning or all-day sickness. She mirrors back to us our blood, which can be soul crushing or soul satisfying. Some of us have even lost our young to the toilet, a big white unintended burial chamber, a chalice of pain and weakness, a vessel that can break a heart. We also might send our beloved pets to a watery grave, surrounding her during a funeral for goldfish and dead mice. We seek the toilet to hide, to be alone with all our fluids. Stolen moments just sitting, scrolling on iPhones, away from little people, needy husbands, relatives, or too many party guests. Sometimes with a cigarette and an open window, or a vodka martini and a notebook. A pill or a line of coke. We sit and read a real book with paper pages with the door locked, hoping the toilet is the one sacred place little hands will be too terrified to knock. We sacrifice our hair to her, cut our bangs, our man's hair, our child's hair, our leg hair. Hair that has been shaved off before cancer can ravage it. It's where we flee to at a party after unwanted advances, our one escape, the one get-out-of-jail-free card. We bring friends, we encircle her in sisterhood, laughter, and tears. It's where we hide to sit and cry at the end of our marriages, flushing tissues full of tears, leaving no evidence behind. When someone we love has died and we just sit in stillness, no fluids left to give.

We lay next to it with our cheeks and bare head on the cool tile of the bathroom floor hugging a towel after chemo, waiting for the nausea to back off. A toilet can stop a woman's heart in the best and worst ways. She takes away all our unwanted fluids, regrets, and decisions and sends them far with an audible flourish. With the push of a finger she flushes the slate clean to help you to forget, to absolve you. She sits silently and waits for our next need to be taken care of. She never judges, but occasionally she shows us our own reflection in her waters. Our true reflections, the ones we can't hide from. The ones we should not be ashamed of. That we should instead be proud of. Like the endless stream of sacred fluids and waters that enter and exit a woman's body, the reflection of one woman is a reflection of all women. The reflection should be a reminder that we are all in this together, in health and in suffering. The toilet is a vessel that never lies yet never speaks. She takes our secrets and shows us our truths and yet has the magical power to erase all evidence without judgment. She forgives. A true porcelain goddess.

Called Home

Repeated frames
Hawk flying
Gray blackness
Like old film
Until
Sun flickers
Into golden amber
Beyond the horizon

I'm driving
Stone pavement
Confusion
Slow motion

I can't move
The house
I can't scream
The house
I can't get home
But I'm here

She is there
Naked
She does not touch me
Softness
She knows the way

It is Sunday
In the city
Beyond the horizon
We are late
I'll miss church

But I am here

Gasoline Shampoo

My father washed my hair in gasoline once when I was eight. Not because I had lice but because a letter came home from school saying that I might have been exposed to it. My father thought he was being preemptive against the little white gnat invaders, but really, he was just too cheap to buy the eight-dollar lice shampoo they sold at CVS. Because a gallon of gas back then used to cost pocket change, or couch change we called it. "There's no way those fuckers can live through this." He laughed after he poured the stinging fumes onto my head, very pleased with himself, still dressed in his janitorial uniform after a day's work.

He laid me down prone, face up to the spring sky on his newly built picnic table, the wood was still yellow and alive. My head is hanging off the edge like face up to a guillotine. A red bucket on the ground beneath my head to catch the runoff for reuse.

My skull was on fire, and I was dizzy with heat, sunlight, and fumes. In my memory it is summer or spring because the backyard is green, and the sky is blue with cotton ball clouds.

I spend all the hot water I can trying to soap up and re-soap my hair in the shower to get the horrible smell out. That week in school I mysteriously lost a bunch of friends for no reason. When I finally asked a girl from the neighborhood why, she said it was because I had been wearing my hair curly and that no one liked my curly hair. As I washed and rewashed my scorched hair, all I could think was that maybe, if I was lucky, the gasoline would magically have taken all the curls out of my hair, and I could go back to having friends again.

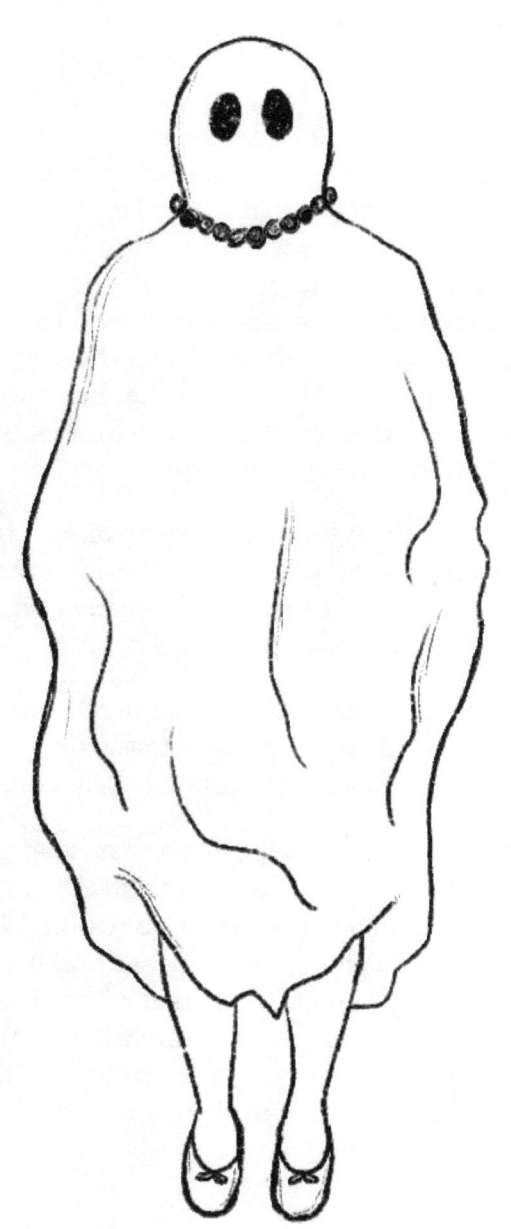

Beheading Pearls

I'm not a thief, but my indifference to letting my youngest sister take literally everything from my parents' house before we sold it started to feel like I willingly handed her a winning lottery ticket. As I watch the furniture, lamps, and ivory mantle tusks all walk by me, I start to rethink my insistence that I wanted *nothing*. I am not nostalgic for any items related to my childhood, despite the grotesque monument my parents built with them. School artwork, locks of hair with pink ribbons, baby shoes, and first communion dresses were all saved, but I'm not flattered by it; my parents were hoarders. They kept everything. We have mail and newspapers in pristine condition from 1985. We just sold 400 sea-glass railroad knobs on eBay that were found in my dad's den. If their plan was to keep us all prisoners here, bogged down by random insulation, then it had more than failed. I saw this day coming decades ago and insisted we sell the house and all its contents as-is, but if my three sisters had the energy to shovel through eras of dust for my mother's beaver fur coat and gold watches and my father's Civil War coin collection, then they could have at it. If I had my way, I would set a match and not even look over my shoulder to watch it burn.

Despite all the warning chemicals my bones and waters dispatched to not be there on the final day that we handed over the keys to my childhood home, I stand in the house I grew up in. It is like watching an accident on the side of the road; I have to look, I have to witness. Maybe it would resolve something in me. Maybe.

As I stand in the living room of our 40-year family home, it suddenly seems so much larger. So much of my life had happened here. That room had seen everything: the bloodshed, the yelling, the babies, the teenagers, the elderly, the good and the bad. I know which floorboards creak so that you can avoid them when you sneak in at 2 a.m. I remember that the people who owned the house before us had no children and a grand piano in this room and nothing else. I remember laying on the rug in front of the TV on sick days watching MTV alone while my parents worked and my sisters went to school. I remember Thanksgivings so full of people that the table formed an L and spilled from the kitchen through the hallway and into this room.

My sisters and I used to start at one end of this room and run full speed to the couch against the far back wall, and whoever could full acrobat backflip onto it the highest would win. My parents had a reproduction of John Singer Sargent's *The Daughters of Edward Darley Boit* that hung precariously over that red imitation-velvet couch. The painting shows four young girls standing in their parents' living room, two in the shadows and two in the light. *Oh, the irony.* The painting would tremble each time our little legs slammed into the wall upon landing a vault. It is a miracle it didn't guillotine any of us. Now, there is only a dirt gray outline around where the painting used to be.

I hear the click of my youngest sister's high heels above me on the second floor and her quick high-pitched nervous voice instructing the movers. She is trying to be polite but also trying to get exactly what she wants done. I don't like walking up the stairs to the second floor. I barely survived being thrown down those stairs once when I was 16, and I don't care to relive it. It's the most vivid memory I have. I can see my round denim knees right up close to my eyes and nose moving at warp speed as I rolled like an armadillo down to the bottom. I know it only lasted a few seconds, but I remember thinking, *I am not going to survive this, there's no way.* Then as soon as it started, I was a starfish on the landing with my neck at a 90-degree angle up against the front door. Like a cloth doll dropped on the pavement. I lay there for a moment as my father stepped over me in a huff, annoyed because now I was a living reminder of what he just did. I remember thinking, *if I had died right now, since no one else was home to witness this, he would have told the police I fell down the stairs, and no one would have said a word to contradict my murder*. I never told anyone anyway. I moved out six months later.

I pace the room waiting for my sister to come down so that we can leave together and sign off on the final inspection. There are a few pieces of furniture that the movers will take to an auction or a Goodwill that have been left behind. A president's desk from some university, a chair from a Vermont craftsman, and a very old Singer sewing machine that my mother adored. I run my finger over the recently polished top and remember sitting at this as a desk as a child doing my homework. I curiously pull at the side drawer to see if it will open, and it does. At the bottom of the drawer is a large piece of beige folded muslin. The kind used to back a quilt. This has to be my mother's. I pick it up and unfold it. Hold it up to the streaming afternoon sunlight of an empty room. Raw cut edges and feathery strings move with the air and dust particles; the breath catches in my throat. I can tell by the certainty of the cut that my mother had touched this fabric. I can smell the detergent she always washed her fabric in before she began cutting. I fold it back up, think briefly of keeping it, but see a flat, completely square box peeking at me from underneath where the muslin came from.

It looks like a jewelry box, and a very old one. I pull it out to examine. It is made of white leather and has brass clasps; it has a little spring lock on the front like the diary I had in junior high. It's heavier than I expect it to be. I run my hand over the cool, cold leather and press my thumb to the spring. The top flies open like a clam shell and unsteadies me for a moment. Laying in a perfect circle on a green velvet bed are my mother's pearls, or should I say, the family pearls. These pearls went through my matrilineal line back to the Civil War. They start at a pure gold oval clasp and get bigger in the slightest plump increments until they reach the one queen pearl in the center and then begin descending again. I realize I haven't been breathing and take a deep inhale. The last time I saw these was when I wore them to my high school graduation. I hear the click of my sister's shoes carefully coming down the steps. I push the drawer shut with my sneaker and close the box. I pull up my shirt, push the smooth leather box under my soft belly and into the front of my jeans, and pull my coat around me.

Two weeks later I am sitting by a familiar lake far away from where I live. It is fall in New England, my favorite season, the season I was born and the season of my life. I call in sick to work, except I'm not sick. I don't tell my husband or my children. After they leave for school and work, I get on the Massachusetts Turnpike and head west. Out into the wilderness. I follow my GPS to a lake that I haven't been to since I was 10. It was the first place I ever felt light, weightless. Maybe because I didn't visit there with my family. I went there with a friend whose name I can't even remember now. But I remember that we spent the week swimming in the bright sunlight. We would swim out to a dock and lay out until our bathing suits dried and then jump in and start all over again. Her parents have no faces in my memory, but I recall their easiness with each other, her mother's hand on her father's shoulder as she poured lemonade before dinner. The two of them singing 80s rock songs together during the drive out. How I slept with no worries for the first time ever.

It's October, and the cabins are empty. The leaves crunch in the trees, and the water is sharp as a knife. I write my name in the wet sand and watch the slow water lap it away. Not my father's last name or my husband's, but my first name, the only name that's really mine, the one my mother gave me. She fought my father over it. I sit in the cold sand and put my elbow on my knees. I pull out the white leather box and just sit staring into the gray hunter green water. I see the remnants of small bare feet footprints next to me, and I feel a twinge in my heart. I smile so big I almost laugh.

I am not an indecisive person. I never was. Even though I think of my no's as yellow not red, because of course a no should be red, right? But not my no's; they are strong and more malleable, like my mother's pearls that I jingle up and down in my hand as I weigh their fate. The pearls hold the blood, sweat, tears, and flesh of all my female ancestors that lived as American women, whatever that meant to them and whatever that means now. I should feel some loyalty or pride, sadness, solidarity, or something in this mother-to-daughter treasure. But I don't.

I finally decide. I put the fine gold clasp and its adjoining pearl between my back two molars. The silk that holds the pearls together is too strong for me to pull apart by hand. I slowly bite down and the sensation of feeling the silk give way, and the pearl slide off, is dizzyingly addictive. I spit the tiny pearl out into my palm, this odd crustacean waste deemed priceless by humans.

I launch it quietly. I throw it as far and as hard as I can into the lake. It is so light and delicate that I can barely hear the plop, but I see it land. Like a fly fisherman's cast, it plops gracefully into the water. I exhale. I feel nothing.

I pull another pearl and this one is tough, I really have to pull it with my teeth as if I am tearing at a steak. This one gets more air and makes a bigger plop. Gone in an instant, it sinks into its watery grave. These pearls. My bones. We are all just here visiting. Why wear each other around our necks? Why do we put ourselves in boxes for preservation? We should all erode in the end, our minerals seeping back into the water. Suddenly I feel hot tears screaming at my eyelids for release. *Oh God, I want to live forever.* But I am not sure if that would be so wonderful or so terrible.

I don't launch all of the pearls into this lake, only those two. To rid myself of all of them at once would be a tragedy. I get back in my car and head home so that I can be there to welcome my boys home from school, my husband from work. So that we can have a hot dinner together and talk about the day. I won't mention the lake. I put the rest of the pearls into a velvet bag and into my underwear drawer where no one will find them. I keep them safe to dispose of at will, when I can't breathe under the weight of my ancestors. When I need to slay ghosts.

The Privilege of Details

I worry about you lately.
Even reclined and relaxed in your favorite chair
I see you picking incessantly
At that scab
Below your right eye.
It's been almost a year now;
You really need to stop
To let yourself heal.

I know all your details
As any woman who has ever loved anything does.
Eyes like the Atlantic in Falmouth,
A few days without shaving and your fangs come in,
White arrows that grow
Down your chin from the corners of your mouth.

My titan for so long,
Cowboy with broad shoulders.
Your collarbone, my cradle of safety
Where the cotton candy smell of your skin
Cured anything, everything.

But recently I've noticed,
You're not as tall as I thought you were,
Your shoulders are a bit sad.
You still smell the same.

We tiptoe around you
On the days when I can tell that the world is a little too much;
I know before you reach the end of the driveway.
I have a look now
That I flash the boys,
It's a pact, it's a code,
It's a warning,

I see the wheels spinning,
Things are changing,
I know things change.
It is hard to look.
Hard to imagine
A world where we no longer know the details.

To be fair.
I know for sure,
That I am not as tall as I used to be.
I measured.
Once, when we were oh so young and oh so tender
You told me, "No one walks like you,
Like a fearless ballerina, your shoulders are always thrown back
And your head held high with confidence,
You are bulletproof."
I found it so endearing that you never figured out
That I was faking it all along.
Trying to hide the damage.
Or maybe you did.
Eventually.
Either way,
I know for sure,
That girl is long gone, too.
To be fair.

Masculinity Fails

I am chronically ill. I tell myself I wasn't always this way, but there is evidence to the contrary. The story I tell is that somewhere along the way life became too heavy for me. All my literary training and that's the best way I can explain it— somewhere along the way I made a wrong decision, and this is where I ended up. The truth looks more like I have been gnawing the flesh of my nail beds since I was about five years old, have never understood what self-esteem feels like, and never had a proper night's rest once in my life. I remember staring at the ceiling of my old bedroom every hour through the night all through elementary school, so I was ill from the very beginning. I wake up every day and feel that my body faces life as if I am a pound of flesh trapped under a mattress, and I have to keep it off me just enough so I can breathe. I'm not a victim, but I know why I feel this way. A traumatic and chaotic childhood mixed with extreme anxiety and ADHD can make some days just plain black. My chronic illness manifests itself in at least two weeks a month of migraine days despite medication. Constant anxiety and clenched muscle tension, as well as hypervigilance, is exhausting and draining. I always know where the exits are in every building, and I prepare for the worst in every situation that comes my way.

As I said, I am not a victim of these circumstances. I feel pride when my therapist tells me I have developed extreme coping mechanisms over the span of my 40 years, and she admires my fortitude despite the unpredictable pitfalls of depression I have suffered. My answer to this is only that I was given no choice. I would love to take a month off to cleanly and accurately take care of my brain and body, but the bills have to get paid and there are little mouths to feed. You have to keep going because if you stop that's when shit hits the fan. A part of me has always felt that I could somehow magically make all this unhappiness and depression and anxiety disappear if I could just have everything

I wanted: to be a successful writer, move to the woods where it is silent, and have enough money to never work again. Easy, right?

For the first 10 years of my life, I kept a secret. I thought I was a boy. I went to Catholic school and dared not speak out loud that I thought the man upstairs with flowy white robes and a fluffy white beard had made a very bad mistake by putting a boy's soul in a little girl's body. It's not even that I wanted to be a boy, I genuinely believed that there had been some mix up. I did not have the vocabulary to describe this, or the therapy yet to know why I felt this way. So I learned to be a chameleon. I adapted to being a girly girl because I looked like one, and I was able to fit in with my tribe because of my looks, but I never FELT like a girl, or how I perceived girls to feel—vulnerable, protected, cared for, respected, light, carefree, soft. I felt masculine, righteous, strong, independent, like a caretaker for my little sisters. For the next 25 years I went about my business being a boy on the inside and a girl on the outside, and not loving myself either way.

~

March 17, 2001 (St. Patrick's Day). After a long night of bartending my senior year in college, I am exhausted. I am dressed as Britney Spears, and my pockets are full of hundreds of one-dollar bills. The irony is that I am still not old enough to drink, and I have a fiancé. A much older guy at the bar has been flirting with me all night and this is nothing new. He stumbles out into the street at closing time and attempts to put his keys into his beautiful new truck he just finished telling me about buying. Something in me feels for him. I don't feel threatened by him even though I should be in a dark alley at 2 a.m. I take his keys and offer him a ride because I couldn't live with myself if he or the truck didn't make it. He smiles strangely and then takes my hands as gently as if they were a child's hands. To this day I remember it so cinematically, as if heralds began playing from the sky. The world moves slowly, and he pulls me close as if we are going to dance in the middle of the street, except he kisses me. I kiss an older man for the first time—a man, not a boy. I have kissed hundreds of boys before. This time my body reacts differently. He smells of cotton candy. I feel his biceps envelop my shoulder and for the first time in my life, I am a girl. For the first time in my life, I am safe. For the first time in my life, someone wants me. Before that kiss is over, I know I will have this man's children. I am currently engaged to someone else, but I have never been more sure of anything in my life. After a D-graded childhood I know I am safe, and every cell in my body falls for this man. It's chemical. I run home and tell my mother it's love at first sight. She tells me I'm getting married and to not fuck up a good thing instead of applauding me for finally feeling real love for the first time. I wish I had told her that I felt like a girl for the first time in my life.

2006. I fall for the whole masculinity-will-keep-you-safe Disney algorithm. I still feel like an imposter as I walk down the aisle in the whitest of white dresses. I marry the opposite of my father—a handsome, faithful, kind, completely capable man who has secrets like me. He chops wood in plaid, brings car engines sitting for 20 years back to life, nothing he can't do or fix, earns a lot of money, and pays off my school loans. Mirrors me in his ambitions of a better life, changes diapers, and pays bills. He doesn't get my poetry, but he reads it and smiles sheepishly.

2007–2020. We live happily and financially comfortable. We raise two boys who turn out to be amazing, evolved, independent, and kind humans. They stop before judgment, and they know compassion. We high-five one night in the kitchen with tears in our eyes when our oldest son tells of a secret good deed he did, saving his money from mowing lawns to buy his friend a bike because the friend was getting bullied when they walked to school. My son was saving the money to buy himself a dirt bike, but he said watching his friend get picked on hurt too much.

He told his friend it was his older brother's bike that he got for Christmas a few years ago and never used; his brother didn't need it anymore. His friend had been really struggling with coming out at a very young age, and my son knew that standing up for him was sending a message to the bullies to back off. The two rode to school together for a long time after.

Our two teens love us and tell us everything. My son's friends come over and revere my husband as the coolest man ever and ask his advice on everything. I beam with pride.

February 12, 2020. Mike gets a small cut under his eye shaving.

March 2020. Global pandemic hits Earth.

April 2020. I notice the cut is still there, odd considering how casually vain and how healthy Mike is about his body and appearance.

June 2020. The cut has opened to a gash and starts to look mean. I ask him about it, and he says he can't stop picking at it. I tell him I get it, who doesn't love to pick at scabs? I write down the date in my journal, but I'm not sure why. I buy him Neosporin and circular Band-Aids and urge him to leave it alone.

March 15, 2023. The cut is now a nickel-sized permanent scar. He starts sleeping on the couch on the recliner end. He snores away with his right index finger attached to his face as if he is thinking. He strokes the sore with his eyes closed like a baby sucking a binky or caressing their favorite blanket. I noticed he went from picking to stroking. I tell him what my shrink had told me about ADHD and self-mutilation, about how I bite my nails down to bloody stubs, that *I understand* that *I GET IT*, he's coping, coping with a mystery.

Mike when I ask him about it: "It's healing, it's fine."

Other strange behaviors begin to emerge. I worry that he isn't even aware of them happening. I try to talk to him about his vaping while sleeping, about vaping while sleeping without even opening his eyes, about vaping while sleeping with me right next to him, mid-snore without even waking up. I ask him about what I now call the scar hole. What do people at work think? Has he seen his parents lately?

Am I ridiculous for not intervening yet writing these words? Is he keeping me safe from something? Is it from worry? Is he sick, does he have a tumor? Will he take his secret to his grave?

March 17, 2023 (23 years after that first kiss). We vacation down the Cape alone and have a night of rest. I tell him I'm worried, maybe we can get him on antidepressants, but most importantly that I love him and that I am here for him. We go to dinner to celebrate. We go to his favorite steakhouse so that maybe he can relax and enjoy himself. He orders a drink, which is rare these days, far from our origin story. We are a little buzzed, and I mention that "the boys' ages are making me sad lately, like really sad and that I guess I am mourning their childhood a little earlier than I thought I would, I mean 16 and 13 are still babies." I'm babbling and see that suddenly he stops, his lips get twisted. I don't like it, he looks like he is going to throw up. He looks up at me and has watery eyes, something I have never or rarely seen. "I don't want to die," he says; he actually whispers sweetly, pathetically. I don't speak in case I spook him. "I've really been thinking a lot about it lately—a ton. I just want to live until I'm like 184, and I just want to be with the boys forever. I just want to live forever." Then he lowers his head in shame and cuts at his steak ferociously. "I know," I whisper back, "I know."

Now I feel guilt for all those years of letting him give me the gift of feeling feminine and safe. I made him the masculine one and never let him feel vulnerable. I had been so wrapped up in trying to find my own identity it never occurred to me that he

49

had been bottled up as well; the cracks were literally starting to show.

A few weeks later, not much has changed. Mike is back to work and ignoring his feelings, and the scar hole grows by the day. One night my oldest son slinks into my room with the same twisted lips his father wore not that long ago. My son asks me, "What's up with Dad?" with an embarrassed flush in his cheeks. He lowers his voice as he asks, me full of worry, and I cover for his father. "He's fine, he's just stressed. I'm helping him deal. He has a lot on his plate." I have lied to my son, and I feel the gash in my chest open like a zipper that's come undone and will tear me in two. I touch my hand to my aching chest and begin to caress it so it will start healing faster, or so I'm told.

Almost Alive

I wasn't born into easy
He left me for the distance
Never fell into the breath

Like a thirsty rose petal
That falls from the almost-gone-bloom
A life sacrificed for a second more of beauty

I almost wasn't sad
Because who am I but another animal

On the edge of extinction anyway
Scoffing at reason like a mother's advice
Here is overrated anyway

Our young chase perpetual youth
Concerned only with being remembered and
Curating an appearance of perfection
Content with being almost alive, age a virus

I make my way by feeling along the edges of this life
Moving blindly forward with both arms outstretched
Trusting the silent orders that rise
From deep deep in my waters

My hands have deep scars, they are the map keepers
The wolf will be here soon
I will meet you at the bottom of the sky

Content with Angel

I drive a beautiful, shiny black hell machine. I don't drive it to impress anyone, I really don't. I drive it to keep the demons away; it's a pressure relief valve. It probably screams midlife crisis, and my two teen boys think I am ridiculous, but I love it. No shame. I get the finger and get cut off regularly when I'm just moseying along following all traffic rules because people assume I'm an asshole with a luxury car. I get it. I'm not really an asshole (well, maybe), but those people are judging a book by its cover. I drive that car because very few things in my life are as simple and make me as happy as I am when I'm driving. Growing up, I had a complicated notion of freedom, as a woman and a daughter. At 16 I scraped together the $480 I earned in a coffee shop over the summer to buy my first car. It was a priceless lesson. It was something I owned; when I was grounded (which was often) my parents could not take it away or leverage it against me. It was my escape when the violence of my household growing up became too much. Today, I drive a beautiful car because it goes really fast and makes me feel free. It is as simple as that. When it is a beautiful day and the wind is in my hair and I'm cruising down an empty highway and Springsteen or Petty comes on, I feel as free and as close to spirituality as I am able.

On one very random and unexciting Tuesday, I decide I've had enough of the stress of slinking by cops with my three-months-past-expired inspection sticker. I know it is only a matter of time until I get pulled over for it. It's not the car's fault the sticker is expired; she's perfect, I'm just lazy.

I fuck off work early and head to a garage near my house before rush hour traffic starts. I've never gone to this one before, but it seems convenient. When I pull in, there are tons of cars in the lot, but no one is around. I see a boy in a gray tracksuit wandering around the parking lot, looking a bit dazed. He's kind of shuffling his feet in a little bit of a dance that reminds me of my glow-stick clubbing days. He is far too young to remember those days. I wonder why he is not in school and figure his parents are in the garage or maybe own it. I'm obsessed with knowing people's stories. I make them up sometimes if I don't know or can't figure them out. I assign people phantom lives. Both bay garage doors are empty, and the silence and sunlight are streaming down onto the concrete. I pull my car up in front of one and park, leaving her running as a courtesy, and to not be an asshole if I have to move it quickly. I'm expecting to be sent packing without an appointment.

The boy starts walking toward me, teetering as he walks like a metronome. It's not the usual confident strut of a young man. As he gets closer, I realize he is not a boy, more of a man, maybe 19, and beautiful. He comes up very close to my door and just smiles peacefully. He has perfect teeth and peach-colored lips. I've already deduced that he works here. "Do you have any open appointments right now?" I ask him, trying very hard to sound nice. He's looking at his crumpled hands, not at me. I don't know if he heard me. There really isn't anyone else around this large garage, and the sunlight is getting very hot for an early spring day in New England. He is too pretty to be the one who actually touches the cars, not a spot of grease on him. I struggle for a moment to tell if he is real or not. The sunlight surrounds him like a halo, and he hovers above my driver's side window. I look around for some sort of confirmation that he is, but there is none.

I am able to examine him further. He pulls his hands up over his heart, looking like a bunny rabbit. His smile is impossibly innocent, and his eyes the shade of green I will surely never see again. Like green sea-foam glass with golden specks. He looks confused, but I realize maybe I have the protocol mixed up. He is waiting and hesitating because I have done something out of order, outside of his usual rules. He has probably learned from repetition or specific instruction, and we both are trying to figure out which steps we have skipped. But he keeps smiling the whole time, his youth in full bloom. His lips move to speak then stop with the slightest whisper. In my mind, I call him Angel. I like to name things to help figure them out. Naming him makes him real to me, whether he is an apparition or not. I realize this beautiful human must have had a brain injury at some point and only my shame stops me halfway through the thought. I'm thinking like such an ableist, and I'm trying to work on that.

Something has wronged or changed this boy. I realize one of his shoulders is much higher than other, which makes him look like he is constantly turned to the right or not facing you when he speaks. His fingers are tensely pulled together, but he flexes them outward often, and he swings from side to side as he talks and moves. But I can see the remnants of him having another life, one where he was as fit and confident as a king, like my two boys. There is nothing more beautiful than the flower of male beauty, the strength and promise of teenagerhood. There is a flicker of a statue in my brain, like TV static. I don't think he was born this way, there are remnants all over him from another time, like a ghost or a shadow tied to his seams. He has dusty brown chai skin and high cheekbones, a thin Roman face, and a perfect nose. He has high and tight shiny brown curls.

He looks into my face with an inquisitive smile, like he is looking at a painting. So young, in the sweetheart of his life. "Yes, yes," he says to me, "I can take you in right now. Please leave your car right here, and you can wait inside. It will be just a few minutes. Just leave your keys and registration on the dash." He sings as he speaks. I create more assumptions: he is the owner's son; he has been given this job by his parents because it is simple, and he is nice to people. A shame to waste such a good-looking kid—I catch and check myself again. Still, I curiously look around for someone, anyone, yet it is just us. It is in the middle of a workday on a Tuesday and in this large garage on a busy street, there are no typical garage sounds. No lug nuts being squeezed off or tightened, zzzzzzzzzt zzzzzzzzzt. No clanking on wrenches or classic rock radio while a man lays under a car singing to himself. Angel walks away, and I put my keys and registration on the dash; I even push the seat all the way back since I am so short, and he will definitely not be able to slide into the driver's seat unless I move it. I shut the door and leave it running. I head to the waiting room of the garage, which has about five broken-in black leather waiting chairs. This thrills me for some reason. I have Tara Stillions Whitehead's new book in my purse, and I'm excited to sit for a minute and enjoy it. It is usually hours to wait for my car to be checked, and usually, it annoys me. But not today.

After reading voraciously for a few minutes, highlighting and underlining the parts I love, he slides around the corner from the garage into the little waiting room behind the desk. "What's your name?" he says, but then he starts to giggle when I smile and tell him. He points to his ear. He is not asking me my name; he is on the phone with someone and is asking theirs. He taps on his earbud and keeps talking. I blush. He leans over the desk to write something, putting his eyes two inches from the counter and the pen between his thumb and three other fingers. I don't know where my car has gone, and I don't care.

I go back to reading. The cool dark of the waiting room has calmed me. I realize that I am smiling though I am not sure why. The seat I'm sitting in is more comfortable than the couch I have at home. I feel so content and want to sit here and read all day. I'm never still. I'm never content in my own house. I do feel content sometimes in the world of men, in their wood shops and in their car garages. For me, there is safety in machines, not bodies. But the feeling of contentment is so strong it stops me. I close the book and sit and close my eyes. I breathe in and feel the cool dark air wash over my face. I could fall asleep. The smile on my cheeks feels foreign and odd. I don't usually smile so much or for so long.

"All done," I hear and then open my eyes. He is back at the desk, and I see him fold my registration and smile at me. *There is no way that happened so fast*, I think to myself. "Thirty-five dollars," he says. I sadly pull all my stuff together and pack my book back into my purse. I'm extremely disappointed that I am not able to sit here for another hour. I give him my debit card, and he runs it through the swipe machine with a dramatic quick swipe and swoosh at the end that I can tell he practiced. He pulls the tape receipt off the machine's teeth with a satisfying rrrrriiiiiiipppppp and then with a finishing flourish, smooths the rolling paper flat and hands me a pen to sign. I watch his beautiful hands with short nails and pink nail beds. I take my time and write my cursive signature in the nicest penmanship I can manage. I smile and set the pen down and look at him smiling as he watches me. His hands are hung up by his chest like a rabbit or squirrel.

"Thank you very much Julie, have a wonderful day and may God bless you." He does a small bow and looks me dead in the eye. He uses my first name, and it sounds strange on the lips of a stranger. I don't remember the last time someone addressed me so directly or even had my name in their mouth. I am ashamed of how sad this makes me feel. It touches me so much that I feel the burn in my eyes. I try to open the door, but I push instead of pull and stumble over my own feet. He just keeps smiling. I force myself to stop moving before I trip. I compose myself and turn my whole body toward him. There is complete silence. "God bless you, too," I say. I don't believe in God or any of that, but I look him dead in the eye when I say it, and I mean it with every cell in my body.

Ghost Ships

In her *New York Times* best-selling book *Tiny, Beautiful Things*, Cheryl Strayed addresses the phantom lives women keep stored in their brains for no one else to see. The lives we could have led if we chose different paths. The lives we regret not living and beat ourselves up about constantly. Strayed so aptly calls them ghost ships, and I can't think of a more suitable name. She says that we should admire the "sister lives" that might have been and accept that they were never meant to be. Strayed adds that the best way to respect but dispatch them is to simply watch and "salute them from the shore." I have been thinking about this a lot lately. In fact, it takes up much of my headspace at the moment. I've reached an age where certain dreams, no matter how small or big, are just not attainable anymore simply because my life span will not support everything I've always wished to become. Yes, I have knocked some out of the park: wife, mother, daughter. But what about the ships I wanted to sail myself, just for me, to define my life?

When I was a child of maybe three or four, my parents used to have me come out in my fuzzy-footed pajamas at parties and ask me in front of their friends, "What are you going to do when you grow up?" My answer, which always evoked an awe or a giggle from the audience and a pat on the head was, "I am going to Harvard." When I was four, I had no idea what or where Harvard was, I just knew that it was the epitome of everything my parents wanted me to be and the thing that would make them most proud of me. When I was in junior high the movie *Top Gun* came out. My parent's mantra of Harvard turned into joining the Air Force. Now when my parents asked in front of their friends, I was supposed to say, "I want to pilot F-14s." My parents wanted me to be a female Maverick. They even went as far as taking my sisters and I on a family trip to Annapolis and Washington, D.C. I saw an actual F-14. I still have a picture of me leaning against it with my arms crossed, dressed in my magenta denim jacket and my bangs sprayed like a ship's sail over my forehead. This is when I realized that my parents probably didn't want me to be myself and that I wasn't in control of my own future and my own dreams. Or if I was, my dreams were just not good enough. I would be defined only by the successes I achieved that could reflect back onto my family.

I have heard that a female child is born with every egg she will ever release already in her womb. If this is true it means that every woman's story began when her mother was conceived back in her grandmother's womb. Every woman is truly the sum of her ancestors. I should be proud of mine. That means I became a whisper to the universe while my maternal grandmother was a soldier and a nurse in World War II, on a continent far from where I live now. That means that I am a piece of a brave 20-year-old single woman in England who left her home country and the lack of religious freedom on a ship called the Mayflower 400 years ago. She would go on to marry my great-grandfather 14 generations back, a young carpenter, have many children, and help found the state of Massachusetts. It has been 400 years, and I only live about 50 miles from where that ship landed. Do I also carry the generational trauma of abusive husbands and fathers, war, and more war? Yes, I do. A psychic once told me I am descended from warriors, female warriors, and she was right.

My parents were both from very poor and not well-educated backgrounds. However, they were both amazing artisans and artists. My mother got into one of the best art schools in the country but gave it up to get married and have kids. She used to make little comics in blue ink on napkins when I was little. I would ask her why she didn't paint me a picture, and she would look deep into her perpetual cup of tea and look very sad; she could never meet my eyes when I asked her. "That was a long time ago," she would say. But then when I was around 10 my mother began quilting. She made everyone these quilts that would rival colonial sewing bees. At some point my mother waved goodbye to the ghost ship of being a traditional artist and became an even more successful textile artist. Now, retired from being a secretary for 30 years, she flies all over the country showing her work. She taught me to quilt, and I am OK at it, but her execution cannot be matched. Her stitches are as perfect as the rings of a seashell. I don't have the patience for a perfect stitch.

My father learned a trade early knowing full well that college wouldn't be an option for him. He was a carpenter. He worked in facilities, maintenance, and carpentry for 40 years. He had callused hands well before I was born. His pride was in a perfect doorframe, a new window expertly set. He couldn't read Shakespeare, but he could cut a perfect 45-degree angle by eye and lay a board without a level. He used to make us toy block sets and toy trains, wooden dolls that my mom made matching dresses for. He went to a few trade shows and tried to sell his wooden dolls until he realized it was just a thing his children loved, and so he let his life as an artisan set sail as a ghost. Like myself, my parents gained their happiness and true worth from creation, from art. But by not being secure in their own skins, they projected their own ghost ships onto my sisters and I.

I wanted to be everything as a kid. I wanted to be Indiana Jones before there was a Lara Croft. I was obsessed with archaeology and traveling the world. I wanted to be a race car driver before there was a Danica Patrick. I wanted to be an Olympic athlete like Nancy Kerrigan. I wanted to be an artist and a college professor. A poet and a scholar. As an adult, I want to be Stevie Nicks, Joanna Gaines, and Maggie Smith.

I inherited both of my parents' love of art. I knew very early that being a painter and an artist was very important to me and that's what I wanted to do with the rest of my life. I got into an Ivy League school based on my painting portfolio. It is one of my proudest achievements. My parents let it be known that they did not support this and that I would not live in their house unless I changed my major to something commercial, something I could get a job with. Since I had won every single writing or poetry contest we had in school, we settled on English.

I spent my late 20s and all of my 30s believing I was a sell out. I was so clear on what I wanted when I was young, and I told anyone who would listen that nothing would stop me. Instead, I graduated and got a job as an administrative assistant because that was the only job for which I deemed myself worthy. I wanted to write the great American novel, but I had massive school loans to pay, as well as rent, so the next few decades slid by with a numbed passivity. I worked to pay the bills and support my children. I was my mother, I was my father; my own dreams took a backseat to family duties.

I married a good man; he encouraged me to go back to school, to write. I leave my short stories and poems printed out on white paper and stapled on the front seat of his truck so he will find them on his way to work in the morning. So I don't have to see him read them. So he can think about them alone without me there, and I look forward to his thoughts when he gets home. We had two amazing children. He has healed so much trauma in me and preconceived notions about men. I learned a man can be a caring father and husband. That teaching boys to be OK with their emotions and that it is OK to be vulnerable just helps all of humanity. My 16-year-old son is six feet, two inches tall, and he will bear hug his shorter father in the kitchen and tell him he loves him every night before he goes to bed, even sometimes in front of his friends. I have to look away when I see this or my heart will explode. They both have become kind and ambitious human beings. When I think of how proud I am of them I get teary-eyed. I hate this cliché, but they are my greatest accomplishment. When I see myself in them, I am happy.

As many women report, when I turned 40 a switch flipped in me. My children were older and more independent, self-sufficient, approaching teenagedom, and needed me less and less. The eternal days of helicopter parenting and hovering to make sure they stayed alive eased up a bit. A global pandemic hit the world and working from home now became a new way of life. For working moms like me, it afforded me the freedom to go back to school and get my master's. If not for the love and care of the female professors I encountered, these stories would not exist today.

So, like I said, some of my ghost ships have sailed, never to return to shore. I will never get a degree in archaeology and go dig in Egypt at the pyramids. I will never find the Holy Grail. I am far too old and out of shape to be an Olympic athlete. As far as being a professional race car driver, I tell my boys I am a domestic race car driver because I love to drive fast. Some of my ghost ships have returned to shore and let me on board; being a published writer and a college professor are all dreams come true. And if you are reading this book, then I am an author as well. I will never fly an F-14, but as for Harvard, I go there every day. I have a job as an administrator there, purely by chance.

I am still that little girl screaming and raising her hand. "Here I am, look at me, I am here! Do you see me?" I have spent my whole adult life waiting to fit in and feel whole. Waiting to feel like I found the "thing" that defines me, that I was destined for. I have not found what that thing is, I don't know anyone that has. I know my children will be the only ones to remember who I really was, and I am at peace with that. I am content with the life that I built. I did not sell out. I just took a few extra and extended detours.

My ghost ships do not go gentle into that good night. My ghost ships are beautiful, they are all different shapes, colors, and sizes. They sail down the river of my life with full flags flying. I stand at the shore and not only salute them, I wave and scream and jump up and down, letting them know that I see them and that they are even more beautiful for having never come to be.

How to Feel a Poem: Instructions

I am five years old and make sure I am silent in the back of my parents' brown 1990 Dodge Caravan. My father turns the radio knob, and a man's beautiful, gravely sad, sweet voice comes through the speakers. I feel like thick, cold, aloe-y hand cream is being deliciously smeared inside my skull, soothing relief for my little brain on fire. His words are like hands that reach down my throat and hold my lungs in a fist. Sound is touching all the yuck that cannot be spoken that I have stored in my belly. It's being squeezed out through my eyes in quiet, salty tears. I feel like I have found out a secret I wasn't supposed to know yet.

He sings about Mary and her dress swaying. I close my eyes and picture her in a white linen dress with tiny white roses, just like my mom's. His name is strange, like the author of the green-covered book about the tree that the school librarian gave me. *This is poetry*, my bones tell me. My baby blond hair whips through the summer wind of the open window, hiding my revelation. I can feel the intermittent sunlight in flashes warming my bare shoulders. I close my eyes and enjoy the smooth speed of the van as the radio plays. I realize I am smiling.

~

Step 1. Sit butterfly-kneed on your twin bed from childhood and pull the sheets over your head to drown out your parents screaming (if not physically, then imagine you are there). Place cherished poetry book you got from the public (school) library across your knees. Smell the paper, the sweet smell of age. Put those pages right up until they touch your nostrils. Just holding this book makes you feel that you discovered a secret of humanity. Try to go back to that feeling.

Step 2. Press play and record simultaneously on your pink and turquoise Yamaha cassette player. Savor that delicious click of the plastic buttons clicking into gear. Close your eyes.

Step 3. Slow your breathing. (Still keep your eyes closed!) Drop your shoulders and tilt your chin up. Flutter your knees a few times like beating butterfly wings.

Step 4. Say your favorite word out loud (or in your head). I use Thunderhead (word is interchangeable). "Thunderhead." Now close your eyes and say it again. "Thunderhead."

Step 5. Think of how in a good driving ballad the lyrics make you feel like an unstoppable yet amazing train wreck. The train cars of words just keep slamming into each other like dominos, Bam! Bam! Bam! blurring lines and creating jutting edges but still urging each other forward. A drumbeat that throws you makes sudden stops and starts and a long steel guitar squeal as the breaks try to stop the driving motion of cars as they move forward into the future, harder and harder.

Step 6. Pull your fists into your sides. Punch forward as you speak each line, speak to the drumbeat. (Punching a pillow can also be substituted.) Feel your spine being strummed like strings, side to side sway, make sure your neck goes with it. It's OK to smile.

Step 7. Slow it down. Place your hands on the sides of your cheeks, palm down. Sing or say "Hallelujah." (Eyes still closed.) Think about how the muscles in your face move as you speak "Thunderhead" (interchangeable). Now whisper it. "Thunderhead."

Step 8. Now let all your favorite words spill out of your mouth like Scrabble tiles until they are stacked or thrown all over the floor, any order, any volume, any treble, for example: Telluride, Eucalyptus, Velvet . . . Bodi . . . Boss, Motor, Revenge.

Step 9. Ring a bell . . . : : : . . . Think of how tender the air is after a bell is rung, how it commands empathy and goodness. No bell has ever rung for evil. Ring it again, just for the hell of it.

Step 10. Press stop. Or just stop. Breathe. Are you in tears? If not, you may want to go back to step 1. If you are, let those salty tears fall, lick them off the side of your face and taste them, wipe them with your index finger and fling them at the wall. They are yours after all, just like words. Tools for exorcism.

Step 11. Grab a pen, your favorite pen, maybe a pencil. Maybe a keyboard. Write it ALL down. On a napkin, in a notebook, on a book cover, on your hand. Now, repeat, repeat, repeat. Go back to the start and repeat it for years if needed, you can even skip steps, until all of the yuck that cannot be spoken, that you have stuffed down to the bottom of your stomach, no longer has power over you.

Step 12. (Insert your own step.)

Julie Alden Cullinane is a neurodivergent poet, author, and mom in Boston. Her first publication was a poem in *The Boston Globe* at age eight; she has been writing ever since. After raising a family and working for many years as a young mom, she was able to return to her graduate studies later in life and earned her master's in 2021. Under the guidance of many amazing and supportive female professors, she began submitting her work for publication. She has published poems and short stories in 20+ literary magazines since 2020. She works in academia full time when she is not writing. Julie's focus of writing is often on the untold seasons and shades of a woman's life. She loves to highlight the dichotomy of the modern pressures on women and mothers between having a successful career and an expected perfect domestic life. Her favorite writers are Eavan Boland and Anne Enright. When she is not writing, she enjoys long naps on the couch with her beloved dog. She is currently knee-deep in a midlife crisis. It takes up all her time. She will definitely be writing about it.

Find Julie online at julie.wildinkpages.com/poetry, on Instagram or Threads @HerLoudMind, and on Twitter or Blue Sky @AldenCullinane.

Thank you for supporting independent publishing.

Yellow Arrow Publishing is a nonprofit supporting writers and artists identifying as women. Visit YellowArrowPublishing.com for information on our publications, workshops, and writing opportunities.